SAS Data Integration Developer (A00-260) Exam Practice Questions & Dumps

Exam Practice Questions for SAS A00-260
LATEST VERSION

Presented By: Quantic Books

About Quantic Books:

Quantic Books is a publishing house based in Princeton, New Jersey, USA. , a platform that is accessible online as well as locally, which gives power to educational content, erudite collection, poetry & many other book genres. We make it easy for writers & authors to get their books designed, published, promoted, and sell professionally on worldwide scale with eBook + Print distribution. Quantic Books is now distributing books worldwide.

Note: Find answers of the questions at the last of the book.

QUESTION 1

Assume that you have completed the Register Tables wizard in SAS Data Integration Studio. Which statement is true?

A.   The physical table(s) selected are copied to the application server specified in the library.

B.   The physical table(s) selected are copied to the SAS Folders location specified in the wizard.

C.   Metadata for the physical table(s) selected is stored on the application server specified in the library.

D.   Metadata for the physical table(s) selected is stored in the SAS Folders location specified in the wizard.

QUESTION 2

You want to register an external file with the following structure: first line contains Customer First and Last Name second line is address1 third line is address 2 fourth line contains the phone number What action should you take to read this file?

A.   Use the New User Written External File wizard.

B.   Use the New Fixed Width External File wizard.

C.   Use the New Delimited External File wizard.

D.   Use the New COBOL Copybook wizard.

QUESTION 3

Registering metadata for an ODBC data source involves registering:

A.   a library that will use a SAS/ACCESS engine to a specific database

B.   only an ODBC data source definition

C.   a server definition that points to the ODBC data source and a library accessing this server definition

D.   a table pointing directly to the ODBC data source

QUESTION 4

SAS Data Integration Studio is dependent on which administration functions?

A. Setting up of SAS Information Map environment.
B. Setting up of SAS Web and SAS Portal environments.
C. Setting up of SAS Application Servers.
D. Setting up of SAS Libraries definitions.

QUESTION 5

The ability to deploy a SAS Data Integration Studio job as a Web service or a SAS Stored Process requires additional set up that is performed in which client application?

A. SAS Data Integration Studio
B. SAS Enterprise Guide
C. SAS Job Deployment Studio
D. SAS Management Console

QUESTION 6

Which of the following is NOT defined as part of the New Library Wizard?

A. the type of library
B. the metadata name for the library
C. the location of the library
D. the metadata for the library tables

QUESTION 7

Within SAS Data Integration Studio, which one of the following is NOT an option available from the File-> New menu choice under External File grouping?

A. Delimited
B. Fixed Width
C. User Written
D. COBOL Copybook

QUESTION 8

Which statement correctly defines a System DSN?

A. Not specific to an individual user. Anyone with permission to access the data source can use it.

B. Specific to an individual user. It is available only to the user who creates it.

C. Not specific to an individual user. It can be shared among users even though it is created locally.

D. Specific to an individual user. But it can be shared among users.

QUESTION 9

In the following display, can status handling be enabled for both the Extract transformation and the Sort transformation?

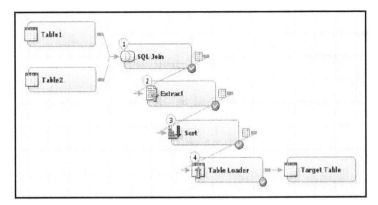

A.   Yes. The Return Code Check transformation can be added to the job flow immediately following the Sort transformation - the Status Handling tab in this Return Code Check transformation properties can then establish the desired status handling for both the Extract and Sort transformations.

B.   No. Both the Extract and the Sort transformations do not have a Status Handling tab in their corresponding properties window, therefore it is not possible to

establish status handling for these transformations.

C.   Yes. The Return Code Check transformation can be added to the job flow twice, once immediately following the Extract, and again immediately following the Sort - the Status Handling tab in each of the Return Code Check transformations properties can then establish the desired status handling.

D.   Yes. The status handling tab in the job properties window will allow you to select which transformation (or even several transformations) that you want to define status handling for.

QUESTION 10

When writing postcode in the Precode and Postcode tab of the
Transpose transformation in SAS Data Integration Studio, which symbol
allows you to reference the transformation output table regardless of the
actual physical name for that target table?

A. &syslast
B. syslast
C. &target
D. %target

QUESTION 11

Consider the job flow diagram in the display. Which of these objects has
parameters defined for it?

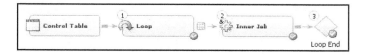

A. Control table
B. Loop transformation
C. Inner Job
D. Loop End

QUESTION 12

You want to create a table containing all customers from Italy. Assume that global customer order information is available in a single table. Identify the SAS Data Integration Studio transformation that will help you perform the task easily.

A. Append
B. Extract
C. Lookup
D. Mining Results

QUESTION 13

In the following display, can status handling be enabled for the Extract transformation?

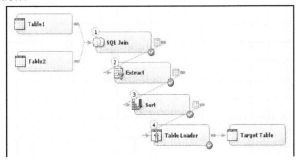

A.   No. The Extract transformation does not have a status handling tab in its Properties window, and the Return Code Check transformation can only provide status handling at the job level.

B.   Yes. The Return Code Check transformation can be added to the END of the job flow - the Status Handling tab in the Return Code Check transformation properties can then establish the desired status handling.

C.   No. The Extract transformation does not have a Status Handling tab in its Properties window, therefore it is not possible to establish status handling for this transformation.

D.   Yes. The Return Code Check transformation can be added to the job flow immediately following the Extract - the Status Handling tab in the Return Code Check transformation properties can then establish the desired status handling.

QUESTION 14

You want to create a job that checks conditions for your data before that data is loaded into a data warehouse. The job should be able to detect error conditions such as missing data or duplicate data and take appropriate actions like registering error conditions in log, etc. Which SAS Data Integration Studio transformation should you use?

A.   Data Transfer

B.   Data Validation

C.   Data Quality

D.   Data Extract

QUESTION 15

Given the table below as a source table for the Transpose transformation in SAS Data Integration Studio:

Name	Month	pay
Lee	Jan	200
Lee	Feb	1000
Lee	Mar	1100
Smith	Jan	3000
Smith	Feb	4000
Smith	Mar	800

In the Options tab in the Properties window for the Transpose transformation, if the columns are assigned as follows: Select columns to transpose (VAR statement): Payment. Select a column for Output column names (ID statement): Month Select columns whose values define groups of records to transpose (BY statement): Name Which of the following tables is a possible resulting target table?

A.

Name	Jan	Feb	Mar
Lee	200	1000	1100
Smith	3000	4000	800

B.

Name	Jan	Feb	Mar
Lee		1000	
Lee	200		
Lee			1100
Smith		4000	
Smith	3000		
Smith			800

C.

Month	Lee	Smith
Feb	1000	4000
Jan	200	3000
Mar	1100	800

D.

pay1	pay2	pay3	pay4	pay5	pay6
Lee	Smith	Lee	Smith	Lee	Smith
Feb	Feb	Jan	Jan	Mar	Mar
1000	4000	200	3000	1100	800

A. Exhibit A
B. Exhibit B
C. Exhibit C
D. Exhibit D

QUESTION 16

Within SAS Data Integration Studio, which type of expression can be created using the Expression Builder window in the Where tab of SAS Extract transformation?
1) a SAS expression 2) an SQL expression 3) an XML expression 4) a constant

A.   1 and 2 only
B.   1 and 3 only
C.   1, 2 and 4 only
D. 1, 2, 3, and 4

QUESTION 17

Consider the job flow diagram in the display. Assume the inner job has a parameter defined specifying a table name. Which statement is FALSE?

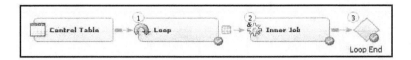

A.   The Inner Job can be successfully executed by itself, but only if the defined parameter has been assigned a valid default value.

B.   The Inner Job cannot be successfully executed by itself unless it is disassociated from the loop job.

C.   The Control Table column is mapped to the parameter defined for the Inner Job using the Loop transformation properties window.

D.   If the server that executes the job has multiple CPUs, parallel processing can be enabled in the Loop transformation properties window.

QUESTION 18

Which of the following is NOT a feature of SAS Data Integration Studio's Data Validation transformation?

A.   The Data Validation transformation can generate match codes to provide de-duplication capabilities.

B.   The Data Validation transformation can perform missing-value detection and invalid-value validation in a single pass of the data.

C.   The Data Validation transformation provides de-duplication capabilities.

D.   The Data Validation transformation provides error-condition handling.

QUESTION 19

In order to use the SAS Data Integration Studio's Apply Lookup Standardization transformation, Data Quality options must be setup. Select the valid Scheme Repository Types. (Choose two.)

A.   A comma delimited flat file that contains the field names in the first row.

B.   Power scheme that is generated by Data Flux.

C.   A SAS table scheme that is generated by SAS.

D.   A third party RDBMS table that has been generated by the SAS system.

QUESTION 20

In SAS Data Integration Studio, which statement is FALSE regarding status handling?

A.   When a job is executed in SAS Data Integration Studio, a return code for each transformation in the job iscaptured in a macro variable. The return code for the

job is set to the least successful transformation in thejob. SAS Data Integration Studio enables you to associate a return code condition, such as Successful, with anaction, such as Send Email.

B.   If status handling has been defined for a transformation or the job, a macro definition (and a call to it)will be added to the generated code to check for the specified condition(s).

C.   Only one Condition/Action pair can be defined for a single transformation or for a job.

D.   The available Condition/Action pairs for transformations and jobs will vary - that is, differentCondition/Action pairs may exist for the SQL Join transformation versus the Table Loader transformation.

QUESTION 21

The Platform Process Manager server is part of the Platform Suite for SAS. Which statement is FALSE regarding the Platform Process Manager server?

A. The server enables you to schedule jobs using a variety of recurrence criteria and dependencies on other jobs,time events, or file events.

B. The server enables you to schedule jobs using a variety of recurrence criteria but does NOT allow you tospecify any type of dependencies.

C. The Flow Manager application (part of the Platform Suite for SAS) can be used to manage already scheduledjobs.

D. Metadata for the Platform Process Manager server must be defined and must include the network address or hostname of a machine as well as the port number for the server.

QUESTION 22

After creating a stored process from a SAS Data Integration Studio job, how can you test the stored process to make sure it runs correctly?

A. Execute the stored process in SAS Data Integration Studio.

B. Execute the stored process in SAS Management Console.

C. Execute the stored process using the SAS Add-In for Microsoft Office or SAS Enterprise Guide.

D. Execute the stored process using SAS Display Manager's Stored Process Test window.

QUESTION 23

Which statement regarding scheduling SAS Data Integration Studio jobs is true?

A.   To schedule a job flow you must first use SAS Management Console to deploy the job for scheduling.

B.   To schedule the job on the Platform Process Manager you require a dependency generator.

C.   Multiple job flows can be scheduled to a deployment directory.

D.   To schedule a job flow in SAS Management console you must first deploy the job for scheduling using SAS DataIntegration Studio.

QUESTION 24

Which statement best describes a deployment directory as used in the Schedule Manager in SAS Management Console?

A.   A folder or directory location on a server where the SAS code from a deployed SAS Data integration Studio job is stored.

B.   A location in the metadata repository where job flows are deployed.

C.   A location in the SAS Management console job directory storing the metadata for jobs that can be added to job flows.

D.   A SAS Folder in the Schedule Manager plug-in within SAS Management Console containing listings of all flows organized by server type.

QUESTION 25

In SAS Data Integration Studio, which component allows the definition of job flows with dependencies between different jobs?

A. the deployment wizard of SAS Data Integration Studio
B. the Scheduling Manager plug-in in SAS Management Console
C. the Scheduling Server
D. the SAS DATA Step Batch Server

QUESTION 26

Which of the following are SAS Data Integration Studio job deployment types? (Choose two.)

A. a Web service
B. a SAS Stored Process
C. a Java Runtime Process
D. a SAS Information Map that is accessible in SAS Web Report Studio

QUESTION 27

A SAS Data Integration Studio job was successfully scheduled and the appropriate event for triggering it occurred. Which statement describes the situation correctly?

A.   The scheduling server calls the SAS DATA Step Batch Server over the SAS Object Server which spawns the job,getting its source code from the deployment directory, and sends the results directly to the Schedule Managerplug-in of the SAS ManagementConsole.

B.   The scheduling server uses the command obtained from the SAS DATA Step Batch Server and the source code fromthe deployment directory to run the job. The results from the executing command are directly sent to thescheduling server.

C.   The scheduling server uses the command from the deployed job in the deployment directory and executes it withthe SAS DATA Step Batch Server which gets the source code from the Metadata Server. The results are sent backto the deployment directory.

D.   The scheduling server uses the command obtained from the Schedule Manager, the source code from SAS DATA StepBatch Server and executes it. The results are directly sent to the scheduling server.

QUESTION 28

Which statement defines the characteristics of a SAS Stored Process?

A. SAS metadata that describes how to collect and store data sources.
B. A document that stores the steps and locations for building a data mart.
C. A SAS program that is stored on the server and described by metadata.
D. A user written SAS PROC step.

QUESTION 29

Which batch server is queried to retrieve the command needed to run traditional .SAS programs having DATA and PROC steps?

A. SAS Java Batch Server
B. SAS DATA Step Batch Server
C. SAS Generic Batch Server
D. SAS PROC Step Batch Server

QUESTION 30

In SAS Data Integration Studio, primary keys, foreign keys and unique keys can be specified/defined in which location?

A. the Keys tab in the properties of a Table Loader transformation
B. the Keys tab in the properties for any transformation
C. the Keys tab in the properties of a table metadata object
D. the Keys tab in the properties of a job metadata object

QUESTION 31

When using the Table Loader transformation in SAS Data Integration Studio to update an existing table containing indexes or constraints, which statement is true?

A.   You can control the removal and/or creation of indexes and constraints in the target table only if you areusing a Load style other than Replace.

B.   You can control the removal and/or creation of indexes and constraints in the target table for all LoadStyles.

C.   If using the Append to Existing load style, indexes and constraints can be added but not removed.

D.   For the Update/Insert load style it is possible to remove indexes not required for the Update/Insertprocessing, but no indexes can be added.

QUESTION 32

In SAS Data Integration Studio, an index can be specified/defined in which location?

A.   the Indexes tab in the properties of a Table Loader transformation
B.   the Indexes tab in the properties of a table metadata object
C.   the Indexes tab in the properties for any transformation
D.   the Indexes tab in the properties of a job metadata object

QUESTION 33

Which statement is FALSE regarding foreign keys?

A.   A foreign key is one or more columns that are associated with a primary key or unique key in another table.

B.   A table can have zero or more foreign keys.

C.   A foreign key cannot exist without an associated primary or unique key.

D.   A table can have only one foreign key defined.

QUESTION 34

Assume that SAS Data Integration Studio Table Loader is being used in a job. The load style selected is Append to Existing. Which statement is true regardingAssume that SAS Data Integration Studio? Table Loader is being used in a job. The load style selected is Append to Existing. Which statement is true regarding this load style?

A.   It generates PROC APPEND code.
B.   It generates PROC SQL code.
C.   It generates either PROC SQL code or PROC APPEND code depending on further option choices.
D.   It generates DATA STEP APPEND code.

QUESTION 35

Select the valid reasons for using SAS Data Integration Studio's Table Loader transformation. (Choose two.)

A.   Create and replace permanent tables.
B.   Maintain access privileges to permanent tables.
C.   Apply and maintain constraints on permanent tables.
D.   Delete and remove permanent tables.

QUESTION 36

Assume that SAS Data Integration Studio Table Loader is being used in a job. The load style selected is Update/Insert. Which statement is true regarding the Assume that SAS Data Integration Studio? Table Loader is being used in a job. The load style selected is Update/Insert. Which statement is true regarding the relationship between the source table and the target table?

A.   From the source table, matching rows are updated in the target table and new rows are added.

B.   From the source table, matching rows AND new rows are added, but the original matching row in the target tableis marked as inactive.

C.   From the source table, matching rows are skipped, and new rows are added.

D.   A or C, depending on further options chosen.

QUESTION 37

When using the Table Loader transformation to load an existing target table that contains one or more indexes in SAS Data Integration Studio, which statement is true?

A.   Indexes are removed when the Table Loader executes and must be re-created using the Table Structure transformation.

B.   Indexes are automatically preserved when the Table Loader executes.

C.   Indexes are removed at the beginning of the load process and must be re-created in a subsequent job step.

D.   Indexes can be removed or preserved at the beginning of the process depending on options chosen. Additional table loader options specify whether to re-create the index at the end of the process.

QUESTION 38

Assume that a SAS Data Integration Studio job is populating a table, and the table has metadata definitions for two simple indexes. Which of the following is NOT a valid location for viewing which columns are indexed?

A.   the Load Technique tab in the Table Loader transformation properties window
B.   the Indexes tab in the table properties window
C.   the Columns tab in the table properties window
D.   the Columns tab in the Details panel of the open job, with the table selected in the job flow

QUESTION 39

Which statement is true regarding SAS packages created in SAS Data Integration Studio?

A.   SAS packages are used to import and export SAS applications.
B.   SAS packages are used to import and export stand-alone SAS programs.
C.   SAS packages are used to import and export third-party metadata.
D.   SAS packages are used to import and export SAS metadata.

QUESTION 40

Which action is required for enabling performance statistics on the executing SAS Workspace Server?

A. Define a logfile for output.
B. Define Collect Diagnostics for the SAS Data Integration Studio job.
C. Define Collect Runtime statistics for the SAS Data Integration Studio job.
D. Enable the logging facility of the SAS Workspace Server.

QUESTION 41

When using SAS Data Integration Studio's SQL Join transformation, which SQL join type can be constructed as either an implicit or an explicit join?

A. Union
B. Full
C. Inner
D. Cross

QUESTION 42

How do you enable performance statistics for a SAS Data Integration Studio job?

A.   Define Collect Runtime Statistics on the SAS Data Integration Studio job.
B.   Define Collect Table Statistics on the SAS Data Integration Studio job.
C.   Define Collect Diagnostics on the SAS Data Integration Studio job.
D.   Define Collect Table Statistics on the SAS Data Integration Studio options.

QUESTION 43

Which statement regarding propagation is FALSE?

A.   Automatic propagation can be set globally, so every new job will automatically propagate.
B.   Propagation can only occur in the direction of the job flow diagram (from beginning to end). Propagation from the end to the beginning is not available.
C.   Automatic propagation that is set globally can be overridden and disabled within a job.
D.   Automatic propagation that is set globally or at the job level can be overridden and disabled for a selected transformation.

QUESTION 44

Within SAS Data Integration Studio's SQL Join transformation, the Validate Expression button is located in:

A. a Where clause definition
B. an Expression Builder window
C. a field Expression definition
D. a Subquery definition

QUESTION 45

Which definition cannot be imported using a SAS Metadata Bridge?

A. Server definition
B. Library definition
C. Table definition
D. Column Definition

QUESTION 46

When exporting a SAS package file using SAS Data Integration Studio, where can it be saved?

A. in metadata
B. on any machine that SAS Data Integration Studio can write to
C. in a SAS catalog
D. only on the machine where SAS Data Integration Studio is running

QUESTION 47

In SAS Data Integration Studio, which output format is supported for the default "out-of-the-box" job report?

A. HTML
B. PDF
C. RTF
D. XML

QUESTION 48

Which statements are true regarding columns when using SAS Data Integration Studio's New Tables wizard? 1. You can access metadata for any column from any table already registered in metadata but cannot change it. 2. You can access metadata for any column from any table already registered in metadata and can override the imported information. 3. You can define new columns for the table. 4. You cannot define new columns.

A. 1 and 2
B. 1 and 3
C. 2 and 3
D. 2 and 4

QUESTION 49

Within SAS Data Integration Studio, automatic mappings are disabled for a job. A transformation has defined source columns and defined target columns. One of the source columns, named COL1, is character with a length of 50. One of the target columns, named COL1, is also character but of length
25. What will happen if the COL1 columns are mapped?

A. The COL1 columns are successfully mapped, one-to-one, with no warnings.
B. The COL1 columns are not mapped because the lengths are different.
C. The COL1 columns are mapped but an expression is defined for the target COL1 that uses a generic specificationof the LENGTH function.
D. The COL1 columns are successfully mapped, one-to-one, but a warning occurs.

QUESTION 50

The profile reports generated in dfPower Profile jobs are viewed:

A.   in dfPower Profile (Viewer)
B.   in the Reports tab of dfPower Profile (Configurator)
C.   in any HTML viewer
D.   in any text viewer

QUESTION 51

A SAS administrator has performed the "Clear Projects" action to remove the lock on a SAS Data Integration Studio job called "Create Tables" that some user has checked out in their project repository. What will be the outcome of this action on the user's project repository?

A.   It will become empty and all new and checked out metadata objects will revert to the not checked out state.

B.   It will only contain the new metadata objects. All checked out metadata objects will revert to the not checked out state.

C.   It will become empty and the DI job called "Create Tables" will no longer be in a checked out state.

D.   It will become empty and will not be accessible until the administrator grants permissions for it to be used again.

QUESTION 52

Which statement best describes the DataFlux Integration Server?

A. An application server that executes service requests based on Simple Object Access Protocol (SOAP) to calldfPower Architect or dfPower Profile jobs.

B. A plug-in to SAS Data Integration Studio allowing you to design jobs specialized for data cleansing operations.

C. An application interface that allows you to build dfPower Architect and dfPower Profile jobs specialized for data cleansing operations.

D. A third party server defined in the SAS metadata repository that allows you to build flows integrating multiple jobs and establishing job dependencies within the flow.

QUESTION 53

The purpose of change management in SAS Data Integration Studio is to manage:

A. metadata objects across metadata servers

B. metadata objects within a logged on user's personal folder

C. metadata objects within a metadata server

D. metadata objects within a logged on user's Checkouts Tree

QUESTION 54

The SAS platform application that can surface the different types of business and analytic content such as information maps, stored processes, and reports on the web browser is:

A.   SAS Information Delivery Portal
B.   SAS Information Map Studio
C.   SAS Web Report Studio
D.   SAS OLAP Cube Studio

QUESTION 55

A user needs to find out who has the SAS Data Integration Studio job "Create Tables" checked out. What action should the user perform?

A.   They need to select the "Properties" menu option and then the "Advanced" tab for the SAS Data Integration Studio job "Create Tables" within Data Integration studio.
B.   They need to select the History menu option for the SAS Data Integration Studio job "Create Tables" once it has been checked in.
C.   They need to select the History menu option for the SAS Data Integration Studio job "Create Tables".
D.   They are not able to find out who has the SAS Data Integration Studio job "Create Tables" in checked out status because they are not an administrator.

QUESTION 56

Within SAS Data Integration Studio, how is the internal code of a SAS Code transformation assigned to its options?

A. SAS macro variables
B. columns of SAS datasets
C. SAS formats
D. SAS macro calls

QUESTION 57

How can you test the interaction of the options of a SAS Data Integration Studio Generated transformation?

A. The transformation has to be used within a job to interactively test the options with the Test Prompt button in the Options window from the properties of the transformation within the job editor.

B. The options can be tested after finalizing and saving the transformation with the Test Prompt item on the Tools menu.

C. The options can be tested only after adding all options that are assigned to the source code with the Test Prompt button in the Options window of the New Transformation wizard.

D. The options can be tested at any time after adding them to the transformation with the Test Prompt button in the Options window of the New Transformation wizard.

QUESTION 58

Within SAS Data Integration Studio, how many inputs and outputs can be defined for a Generated transformation?

A.   A transformation can have zero or more inputs and exactly one output.
B.   A transformation needs at least one input and at least one output.
C.   A transformation can have zero or more inputs and zero or more outputs.
D.   A transformation needs at least one input and exactly one output.

QUESTION 59

How can you make a SAS Data Integration Studio Generated transformation option required?

A.   The name of the option has to start with _REQUIRED.
B.   The type of the column has to be defined as Required Data source column.
C.   The option can be marked as Requires a non-blank value.
D.   It is not possible to make an option required.

QUESTION 60

The SAS Data Integration Studio SCD Type 2 Loader transformation performs which of the following?

A.   Loads source table records into a standardization table.
B.   Loads dimension table records into a fact table.
C.   Loads source table records into a dimension table.
D.   Loads fact table records into a multi-threaded table.

QUESTION 61

In SAS Data Integration Studio, source table records and dimension table records are combined for output using which transformation?

A. Data Validation
B. Lookup
C. DataFlux IS Job
D. Table Loader

QUESTION 62

In SAS Data Integration Studio, surrogate and retained key values are:

A. generated by the Lookup transformation
B. copied from source tables into dimension tables
C. generated by the SCD Type 2 Loader transformation
D. copied from dimension tables into source tables

QUESTION 63

A fact table is populated by using which transformation in SAS Data Integration Studio?

A. SCD Type 2 Loader
B. Data Validation
C. Lookup
D. DataFlux IS Job

QUESTION 64

When using the SCD Type 2 load method in SAS Data Integration Studio, which statement is true when a change is detected?

A.   the old record is deleted and the changed record is added
B.   the old record is updated with the new values from the changed record
C.   the old record is flagged and the changed record is added
D.   the old record is merged with the changed record

QUESTION 65

In SAS Data Integration Studio, the default values for generated surrogate and retained keys contain which type of values?

A.   Date time values
B.   alpha-numeric values
C.   binary values
D.   integer values

QUESTION 66

In SAS Data Integration Studio, the SCD Type 2 Loader transformation will do which of the following?

A.   find row matches using the business key
B.   find row matches using generated cluster numbers
C.   find non-standard values using a generated key
D.   find non-standard values using a business key

QUESTION 67

In SAS Data Integration Studio, where must the columns included in a business key exist?

A.   in the source and standardization tables
B.   in the source and dimension tables
C.   in the target and fact tables
D.   in the source, dimension and standardization tables

QUESTION 68

Which action is performed by the Lookup transformation in SAS Data Integration Studio?

A.   combines rows from multiple tables into a single row
B.   combines rows from multiple tables into multiple rows
C.   validates that values are unique
D.   validates that values are not null

QUESTION 69

The SAS Data Integration Studio SCD Type 2 Loader transformation can do which of the following?

A.   generate cpu statistics
B.   generate a date time value
C.   generates cluster numbers
D.   generates standardization values

QUESTION 70

When using the SCD Type 2 load method in SAS Data Integration Studio, which columns can be selected to check for changed data?

A. business key columns
B. Type 1 columns
C. generated columns
D. non-key columns

Answers

1. Correct Answer: D
2. Correct Answer: A
3. Correct Answer: C
4. Correct Answer: C
5. Correct Answer: D
6. Correct Answer: D
7. Correct Answer: D
8. Correct Answer: A
9. Correct Answer: C
10. Correct Answer: A
11. Correct Answer: C
12. Correct Answer: B
13. Correct Answer: B
14. Correct Answer: B
15. Correct Answer: A
16. Correct Answer: C
17. Correct Answer: B
18. Correct Answer: A
19. Correct Answer: AC
20. Correct Answer: C
21. Correct Answer: B
22. Correct Answer: C
23. Correct Answer: D
24. Correct Answer: A
25. Correct Answer: B

26.   Correct Answer: BD
27.   Correct Answer: B
28.   Correct Answer: C
29.   Correct Answer: B
30.   Correct Answer: C
31.   Correct Answer: B
32.   Correct Answer: B
33.   Correct Answer: D
34.   Correct Answer: C
35.   Correct Answer: CD
36.   Correct Answer: D
37.   Correct Answer: D
38.   Correct Answer: A
39.   Correct Answer: D
40.   Correct Answer: D
41.   Correct Answer: C
42.   Correct Answer: A
43.   Correct Answer: B
44.   Correct Answer: B
45.   Correct Answer: A
46.   Correct Answer: B
47.   Correct Answer: A
48.   Correct Answer: C
49.   Correct Answer: D
50.   Correct Answer: A
51.   Correct Answer: C
52.   Correct Answer: A
53.   Correct Answer: C
54.   Correct Answer: A
55.   Correct Answer: C

56.   **Correct Answer: A**
57.   **Correct Answer: D**
58.   **Correct Answer: C**
59.   **Correct Answer: C**
60.   **Correct Answer: C**
61.   **Correct Answer: B**
62.   **Correct Answer: C**
63.   **Correct Answer: C**
64.   **Correct Answer: C**
65.   **Correct Answer: D**
66.   **Correct Answer: A**
67.   **Correct Answer: B**
68.   **Correct Answer: A**
69.   **Correct Answer: B**
70.   **Correct Answer: D**